THE
PRICE
OF A
SMALL
HOT
FIRE

OTHER WORKS

Fiction

Ghastly Tales of Gaiety and Greed: Unauthorized and Haunted Cedar Point

Liar: Memoir of a Haunting

As Fast as She Can

In Trouble (co-editor)

What Happened Was Impossible

Poetry

The Hunger Tree

Chapter Eleven

Judy Garlad is Not a Sunrise

Published by Raw Dog Screaming Press
Bowie, MD
First Edition

Cover art by Steven Archer

Book design: Jennifer Barnes

Printed in the United States of America
ISBN: 9781947879614

Library of Congress Control Number:
2023937980

RawDogScreaming.com

THE PRICE OF A SMALL HOT FIRE

Poetry by E.F. Schraeder

RAW DOG
SCREAMING
PRESS

For all motherless children and our distant mothers—you are seen, you are complete, you are valued

CONTENTS

AUTHOR'S NOTE

Here's the introvert's dilemma: How might I best contextualize a collection of poems that nearly ripped me in half?

From a nice safe distance, that's how.

Like horror, poetry is often personal. Both are immediate, unruly, and full of nerves. As I sit writing this note, I can't help but reflect on my experiences talking with readers and how many times I've heard many people admit, as if under some unseen pressure, that they'll read anything but horror or anything but poetry. Horror and poetry might be disliked in equal measure, but I've had a bad case of love for horror and poetry since I was a kid. I loved entering the imagined world of words and images, being jolted by brief sharp insights and shocked by sometimes twisted resolutions. For a kid who experienced some trauma (an intentionally vague admission), these twining interests co-evolved and persisted unapologetically. Poetry isn't therapy, but it can be highly personal. The word personal suggests true, and that gives me pause. How much do I say about what frightened me over the last few years in writing these poems? Too much, and it sears my edges. Too little, and it's impersonal.

Horror poetry, like other horror media, provides a path to explore what frightens us with a distance that affords safety. In the course of a few phrases and images, the horror poem invites readers through a variety of dangers and shattering losses, often with an unflinching clarity. As many poets who've come before me have noted, there's no set meter or form and no special requirement of topic or style for a poem to qualify as "horror." No topic is off limits. Whether understated or blood-soaked, a horror poet's personal take and artistic license may yield an intensity of pitch or punch that offers unusual or uncomfortable discovery, but there are no rules (and if there were, most poets would probably break them anyway).

The subject here may be personal, but to my thinking a reader's interpretation is as powerful as a poet's intent. Like a camera obscura, the images rendered in the dark chamber of this collection offer up a reversed picture that's up for interpretation. What's true? None of it. All of it. Something in between.

Under the largest umbrella, the following poems are about complicated grief, responding to the death of an estranged parent. A mother. (Such a distance of those words! Not "my mother," but the indefinite article). But the unexpected, nightmarish truth that scared me more than my mother's impending death was my openness to engage with someone who had written me out of existence. The tense connections between mother and child don't simply blow away like dust but sink in like wet charcoal stains. Mothers have long been made monstrous, judged and (de)valued for any number of decisions they make, things done and undone. I know mothers are too-often rendered with an unflattering or one-dimensional lens. This isn't one of those endeavors.

Sometimes I think of poetry as a place. I wonder if I might prefer to live there, and if in some ways I already do. The poems tell a story of estrangement and loss, fear and resilience. Like other art forms, poetry has a vulnerability. In telling any particular story through verse, particularly horror verse, there's risk. I tend to think poetry lives on the nerves, and these poems, I hope, are no exception. How people grieve or don't when someone dies is a deeply personal matter, but death, like poetry is about how to grasp it. Life is full of poetry and horror. It's up to any of us how closely we choose to look.

AFTER BIRTH (INTERIOR NEEDLES)

Mother chanted a bitter blessing,
cinched my twitching arms with one hand.
Sternum to clavicle, she sliced my slick flesh
with a thumbnail sharp as shears.

She pressed her lips to a bundle of thistle,
then planted the spiny web within me,
deep in the cavity that held my heart—
nested like tiny daggers of teeth.

With fingertips dabbed in mud,
she pinched the edges of gored flesh,
knit my chest shut like a pie crust,
pressing until my skin held the seam.

The stinging subsided, the wounds
healed smooth. Light as freckles.
An unnoticed series of stains
she named a protection.

The spell set well as I grew,

inching into her careful interior needles,
memorizing love's lesson—
the stab each time I dared to want.

POSTMARKED FROM NOWHERE

Once she was the mother of all my edits,
each judgement landing like an underlined phrase.

She inserted commas into adolescence,
until I craved erasers and disappearing ink.

Deadly sharp, her red pencil of a finger managed mistakes,
framed my edges, circled problems. Crossed out errors.

I sketched a decade, then two in powdery charcoal,
left white spaces where relationships could go.

I sat with blurry gaps, stared at blank pages of a life,
not ever and somehow always missing her, the empty mantle

for the contented paragraphs of a family.
Then her handwriting appeared in my mailbox,

A note that said not sorry,
but hello.

UNINVITED WELCOME FRIENDS

Standing on the doormat, a strange face smiled,
half recognizable over the guarded shell wall
of memories stacked between us.

Part of me hid, withering. A clumsy child
at Pandora's door. Trained in acrobatic self-deception,
I froze, a worried grin stretched my lips.

We stood between snowdrifts on the porch
and talked, shivering in December's air.
A cold waited between us.

Cold because our past has no wings.
Cold because we are non-convergent,
branched trees, and alike in this way.

Call me, she says. I think I won't, know I will,
and when I do, *We could've been*
becomes a chorus for breaking apart.

CONFESSIONS OF AN AVON LADY'S DAUGHTER

Charcoal pencil lines the tender skin,
I feel naked without makeup, she says.
  I watch her become herself in the mirror.

One fingertip smoothes the line, blurring for effect.
I never go without mascara. The whole bit.
  Very pretty, I think. *I'd like to learn,* I say.

Her lantern eyes probe me. She shakes her head.
No. I don't want you to feel like that.
  I never learned.

ALTERNATE WORDS FOR ESTRANGED

Waking in a brittle aftermath of flooding memories,
even I struggle to believe

such disintegrating isolations of silence—
a high-wire mile without nets.

I plucked recurring nightmares like invading weeds, flung
them to the scorned realm of my unconscious

beneath layers of ice so thick I froze, stunned
by the quickest glance in their direction.

Doctors summoned, directions ordered, decisions made—
all without consent. Naturally, I learned to prefer

the feel of stone. So I reconstructed myself as Defiant Queen,
a monster whose endless winter was not a metaphor.

EMBARRASSMENT OF SCARS

We sing our bitter belated reversals,
and my confused body makes mistakes.

Staggering seems like a run,
falling becomes a plan,

hate feels like love. I swerve
against a crisis of her curves.

Even a late escape teaches me
how to crack myself in two.

Crooked and clawed, I take my time,
wiry restraint carved into my amygdala,

the inherited trauma of her opinions
inked my skin like tattoos.

HOW TO AVOID FEELING

Once I jumped deep into a safe, dark well,
hid in a shadowy cavern, shivering.

I quieted myself with labels and diagnoses
that made sense of the pulsing panic, chaos, dots of light.

I climbed and scraped a path with bleak, bloody hands
like a terrible shadow, risking the stony climb to flee.

I vanished, barefoot, into the listening heart of trees,
waiting for roots to console the softness of my feet.

I've consumed and denied more and less than I need,
lit fires, burned my crumpled intentions like spells,

chain smoked my lungs into charcoal,
sliced into muscle with weights and blades,

poured myself into colorful bottles,
plunged fists into crumbling walls,

put life on pause to confirm
there was nothing so terrible as myself.

Alone, I sucked in air thick with sticky silences, moving
like a click beetle convinced I could right myself with twists.

I'M NOT AFRAID OF

Most things
like being alone or quiet
or chased.

The truth is, most things
don't frighten me at all.
I like jump scares

that punch and kick
like a controlled series
of shock treatments.

I like small spaces, strange places,
unknown faces, and the sensuous rush
of standing on the edge of cliff.

Such things as these deliver exquisite jolts—
relief from numbness. It's comfort and
known entities I shrink from.

The Price of a Small Hot Fire

Because the dark has always been kind to me.
Because of love, I know the best disappointments,
how what's closest can crush or kill you.

LAVENDER MAYBE

She smelled like smoke, old wood, and coffee,
some kind of hippy soap. Lavender, maybe,
an occasional splash of herbs. An earthy perfume
like early dusk and amaranth.

Home is a place I don't remember
and search for like a hero might,
but my quest is selfish, narrow and small.
Uneventfully narcissistic.

What might weaken the things that scare me most?
I make a short list. Identify pros and cons.
Needles and know-it-alls, judgments like knives.
In the garden, I plant the cure for everything.

HURRICANE PANTOUM - FOR FRANKENSTEIN'S MOTHER

How deep the water of a soul must run—
thick muscles thrust through muck.
Each labored word spoken a tribute to my
obsessive, skilled mother's plunging hands.

How she pulled muscles from muck,
delivered a lifeless body to an elevated form.
Obsessed, those plunging, skilled hands
forced open a hurricane heart,

elevated a once lifeless form. Delivered
and lost, her monster trembled,
breathed with the fury of a hurricane's heart.
No one heard when her world exploded.

Lost, her monster trembled,
spoke each word like a labored tribute
no one heard. When she exploded from the world,
one soul sank into the deepest water.

I NEVER SAID

I
overreacted

I
over
reacted

I
over re acted

BARELY MANAGEABLE BONFIRES

I light a backyard burn,
and we linger for hours
over small conversations.
Crackling, nothing ignites.

We sit for many and not enough nights.
Each visit, our words spark late among
the fireflies whose zips of hope
punctuate our pauses with tiny bursts of light.

These fires don't roar but simmer
because I learned from her about
patience, oxygen,
and control.

PINPRICK

More slice than knife
more verb than noun

I grab the edge of the wound
stem the bleed

but quickly
forget the plans

I made to be strong
and alone

without her
as usual

her who I can't
forget loving

DON'T LEAVE

Something recognized,
a flash of green in her eyes.

The first gaze I ever matched.
A laugh. The timbre of the first voice I heard.

Something about how we love bees,
plant clover, adore weeds.

Something scent or cellular
in the messages of neurology.

An inexplicable cadence
of likeness or alikeness.

When I add a branch to the fire
without asking her to stay. She smiles.

I make tea, set cookies on a plate.
Fetch a blanket for her shoulders,

a cushion for her chair,
a treat for her dog.

Don't leave,
my gestures plead,

and I see we might have missed something
like each other these many years.

But being identical,
we admit nothing.

BASELINES AND BORDERLINES

I learned about insecticides
and self-destruction that same summer

passing between first and second base.
An ant hill exploded with small lives,

easy to ignore or stomp out.
I glanced away, stared

at a bed of forget-me-nots off the field.
Better to let them live untouched.

Strike one. *Don't tell anyone.*
What if it doesn't get better?

What if effort sleeps through most days?
Why does the idea of a full stop bring relief?

Hope's pure bright voice muffled
amidst the cheering parents. Strike two.

Third base beckoned. The pitch—
soaked in panic-sweat isn't relatable.

No one's a protagonist if I don't run.
Move! Empowerment is just a word.

Exhausted and unnoticed, I ran.
The odds were against making it.

Happy endings withered, pinned, struggled—
I slid, dust scattered, shins scraped, but safe.

ORIGIN STORY

I was a loyal child of fists and hard forgiveness,
unplanned and bumping on a stony path.

I blossomed into a treasure map of triggers
and missed connections.

I learned this roadmap consisted
of mostly missed exits and detours.

I leapt over each sidewalk crack,
my youth spent on checkerboard moves

in the chess of childhood
where I always lost.

I'M THINKING ABOUT REPETITION

about raindrop moments almost too pattering to remember
about the gray fog year stretching between hellos and stiff hugs
about thirty handwritten notes and her wobbly script
about packaging chocolates and copying recipes
about trips to the post office between doctor appointments
about a clause of time
about a figment, the filigreed loop of us
about an unstoppable catch, a disease's drumbeat
about invention and emptiness
about without
about spiraling loss like smoke I can't hold
about glacial disappointment
about other years
about weeding strawberry patches and asparagus
about homemade bird feeders and bee houses
about puzzles and Joni Mitchell records
about word games and long drives
about easy conversation and laughter
about eager hellos and hollowing goodbye
about waiting and absence

The Price of a Small Hot Fire

THINGS I HAVE DONE TO FEEL

Someone else's chords, plucked
until emotions bruise and bruise—
pain is a song on repeat,

a crescendo of gasped breaths,
bursts of buried years.
Tears are a strange companion

after all this time.
Spread photos on the floor,
punched into memories

where gray spots blur my sight
until the choked sob tells me
if I'm not careful, I could crash here.

FORGIVENESS SPELL

At a barstool, I lean in to remember love,
the action of it. But that's a lie—

I'm always looking at unrecognized faces,
searching for someone to hold against the light

of a well-crafted metaphor or anonymous night.
Someone to fill in the gaps, spark more than memory.

The farthest object we see are quasars in the sky.
Like looking back in time. Or ahead. I see them tonight,

a lifetime of light dispersed into what we call constellations.
Our bodies reinvent themselves through cell division.

Reparations. Is loss so different than love?
To escape the maelstrom, we reignite. Causal certainty.

I digress. A decade of adulthood blinks. More.
Ice clinks in the glass. I lean over the counter

wearing her shirt. Order her favorite drink: chilled, no ice,
two straws. Inhale. I breathe in what she liked best—

the stardust of memory
so pure I can taste it.

FRIENDS QUESTION MY LACK OF ANGER

This hardwiring
never updated to overwrite
the hundred thousand smiles,
the fists I couldn't protect her from,
or the million other reasons like being alive.
So I plan for getting lost in the triage of grief.
Showing up will require a certain confidence in pain.
Anyone could predict that much.

The slices of her will fade me, trip me
on this sandy staircase. I'm a losing grip
on the slick handrails of her unwritten rules.

My good experiment of absence
blocked conflict, carved safety,
perfected boundaries defined by need and fear.
Alone felt simpler, easier to confine.
I shaped myself into a function of her need.

A golem.

But now I am a retreating list of ignored feelings
waiting to fill a vase with tears.

CLOAKED

No clocks keep watch on this restless sleep
while she wrestles with wires and tubes.

Her life reduced to a singular emergency of breath,
a strangled cough of possibilities.

Without kicking or cursing— by choice
I drove to the hospital for this moment

then stood there, shrinking.
The kind veil shimmered

between us: life and death.
Afraid of her papery skin.

Afraid of an absence I couldn't fathom.
In her sea of disappointments,

perhaps I was plankton.
A microscopic irrelevancy.

Absence and anger favorable to this abyss—
this night of no shadows,

this room I could not leave.

THINGS LEFT UNSAID (ANALOG)

Why
          I missed you

Oh
          I missed you too

Why
          I missed you

Did
          I miss you

So
          missing you too

Much
          Missing you

Time
          missing you

Pass
          miss you

Without

   More

RETURNING TO NARNIA

When the child returned with tales of such a trek
through the wardrobe into an enchanted tundra—
how her parents wept!

Poor girl, what's happened?
How have we wronged you?

Strange to ignore the pine needles littering her hair,
to skip over clumps of ice on the floor,
to blink out her sopping wet slippers. Curious,
how they mistook the smoky scent of that checked robe.

Easier to suspect stolen cigarettes. Better to doubt and deny
this hearth-tale of evenings with a cloven-footed friend,
to resist stories of thicketed visits to the netherworld,
the kindness of speaking to beasts. They'd never admit

their stunning neglect.
But imagine, she was gone for weeks. Months. Years!
Enduring conquests, meeting challenges, grieving tragedies.
All while they slept.

SHE WHO MADE ME

Beneath the cool, pale skin sang an electric pulse
so near life—but no warm blood hummed.

Crying, *not of my hand,* her maker fled.
Can a butcher be shocked by blood?

She watched for signs of another presence
in the pinewoods, eyes tracing winks of starlight,

ears attuned to owl calls and winter's breeze.
Her world coiled into an ocean of fears.

Then she became a forest to wander. Betrayal
carved, she forged an empty landscape into home.

She left this patchwork life, stolen and bruised,
her body a mass of swollen, stitched dreams.

With the language of loss caught in her throat,
she became unlucky, a stumbling savior of loss.

When her fingers brush a stranger's hair,
soft tendrils clench in a fist.

So reduced, she learned how to love
like venom.

Hush now. Be still. She knows the secret—
one is not born a monster, but becomes one.

FORGOTTEN CHILDREN & THE WOODS OF DISAPPROVAL

I unlearned the soft rain rhythm of our unfriendly hush,
the icy road of lost invitations and greetings.
We stumbled onto strange paths, trudged un-groomed trails,
each step a steely stab of misbegotten instincts.

I ignored labyrinths of casual warnings,
the dead-end, well intended pleas of friends,
their wayward words about resolutions, hopeful signs,
unbreakable magnet bonds, and other fairy tales.

I overlooked what went missing, learned
to plant kindness amidst insecurities,
to grow love like wildflowers.
Welcome or not, we bloom.

She returned, of course, late autumn,
as winter's chill took hard hold,
when I was no fledgling blue jay or stray mouse
and no delicate eyedropper dared return me to wild.

FOR DEATH

One day
if you are

supremely lucky
you will be nothing

save a picture
on a mantle

NOT ENOUGH (PLATITUDES)

Open the funeral book to the last page.
Read backwards to unlock a spell of lies
engraved and initialed, dated and stamped
in the blood of lost memories.

Empty compliments ripple on pages
soaked with tears and mud.
Each testament to life an inverted
comment about all we erased.

To bury this book,
I sprinkle thistles on the pages
scattered like eyelash wishes
and dig.

PICTURES

Scattered across the living room floor,
I order a chronology of life
arranged to ignore the missing years.

Cupped in her arms,
laughing in a pile of autumn leaves,
perched like wards of the forest behind us,

I find a mother embracing a child,
sharing indulgent, kind pauses,
both unaware how the future may yet betray.

A gaping blank spot between before and after—
where snipped time sings like razors on skin
an invisible wound bleeding out from regret.

STICKS, STONES

According to rumor, I caught fire once
by accident—
lanky limbs flickering to life in flames.

Of course, that's impossible.

This body's arsenal of injuries
sings blue with bruises
long before the explosion.

My skin, so decorated
with history, pinches and punches
into knots worn like sacred stones.

Tell me again how I remain
unextinguished.
My extinction was overdue.

I required assistance.
Self-immolation was an
act of love, not terrorism.

Of all the seeds and sticks,
the mud she collected to build me,
only the heart combusts.

NECESSARY TOOLS FOR THE REINVENTION OF A RELATIONSHIP

Erasers for time,
scissors for pain,
glue for re-assembly.

Matches for memory,
needles for distraction,
thread for alterations.

Safety pins for eyes,
buttons for mouths,
rags for cleanup.

One crystal vase
to hold my tongue
while I listen.

MOTHERS AND MONSTERS

That hatched disaster wasn't what she wanted.
She imagined rooms full of rose-blossoms or giraffes,
delicate dancing mobiles and balloon-parties, candles and cake,
luscious pastels, and sweet planned surprises.

What she got was a mess of too many voices and howls,
too many glittering colors. Something blurry
made all of fingers. Such a hungry, toothy mouth.
A wobbly blobby squirming prism of frightening need.

Something more than human, but nothing recognizable.
Except maybe around the eyes— where the soul hides,
if there's one inside at all. She feared the strange arrival.
Little monster, where'd you come from?

LIFE IN FRAGMENTS

People often miss what isn't seen— the pip
that sits deep within, where old secrets burst.
Sunken. Even she doesn't remember. Time splices.
Deep breath. This will pass. This should have passed.

Pretend it never happened. Memories like clouds pop.
Too young, too timid to know better. Well taught,
she tells no one about anything. She thinks
denials work better, quiet as the dead.

Pain? No, she's just overwhelmed. A wimp.
Trust? Not with that family of hers, that
still silence of theirs about her 'decisions.'
Dating a girl? No thank you, they said.

Panic pricked, sweaty hands, her heart a clamp.
Tense and tight, each muscle a punch. That
started before she had words for it. No label fits.
Drowned in insomnia. Her insides dead.

Petrified, she doesn't look. Plan. Avoid. Jump.

Tired by twenty-two, she fantasized escapes, a twist.
Suicide, strangers, sex. *Say something,* she pleads.
Disoriented, doodling, distracted. Her edges hard.

Pliable neurons rewire for repair. She looks up.
Tries therapy. Treads water. Teaches herself to uncorrupt.
Salvages self care. A fish against current still swims.
Don't give up. Don't give up. Maybe she's not doomed.

BRIDGE ICES BEFORE ROAD

Two ways to get there from here. Both indirect.
I'm wrong roads and missed signs.

Two ways to get there, but the roads split.
I'm lost directions, the failed GPS.

Two ways to get there from here, but it's foggy.
I'm out of the way.

Two ways to get there, but the pass is narrow.
I'm the patch of road folks ignore, drive around to avoid.

Two ways to get there from here. It's hilly, so buckle up.
I'm a mess of curves.

Two ways to get there, but it's impossible to see in the dark.
I'm the unexpected shoulder tugging you off-road.

Two ways to get there from here, both take you to the same place.
I'm what you can't plan for it. Can't avoid.

TRIMURTI - FOR DR. FRANKENSTEIN

An ear at the collarbone, like Brahma
she listens for her creation's absent heart.
Sussing out the sounds of a broken body,
she pieces it together with lies and string.

Sudden as lightning, the husk moves,
shadowy limbs lurch and loom.
She shrieks, terrified but bold, seeing how
the seams of such a face could inspire fear.

Vishnu's perverse effort preserves the thing—
breath enters a soulless life. Only a true genius
can attest: how the body feels so like a tomb,
a gathering place for the mud of life, the sorrow.

Then like a hovering cloud, the monster's dreams
meet daylight, flail to life. Anger bursts
as the thing touches only what can be torn apart.
Oh, Shiva turn this house to ash.

ONE WAY MIRROR

When I look at myself, I see another face—
but the angles are off, stretched
like someone with cheeks full of stones.

Her eyes locked in my sockets,
staring back as if to remind me
I'm being watched.

Like an experiment, sometimes
I move into her familiar expressions,
feel them before I see how they emerge.

An eyebrow, the upward tug of a lip.
I pull her sweater around my shoulders and ask,
when did this stop being my face?

THINGS NO ONE SAID

I m(eant to)
s(ay)
or
(maybe I just forgot to t)ry.

I'm so r(eally ve)ry.

I'm sor(t of not okay
and still ang)ry.

I'm s(tubb)or(nly invested
in eve)ry (word)

I (never heard) am
(maybe not) sorry.

I AM AFRAID OF

The soft squelch of a small spirited wish
like a dandelion petal blown into air.

The sprout of a seedling too fragile to thrive,
too soft for the gentlest breath of cold.

The cruelty of human hands that take
without notice, without care.

Becoming a precious hell, the anecdote
to everyday kindness.

That pinch of delight swallowed with power.
When she told me I wasn't good enough.

Vulnerability.
How much being seen crushes.

CHERRY BLOSSOMS (MOURNING A DISTANT MOTHER)

I sat so long on this bench we made of silence
that I have forgotten how to move. Waiting for spring,

the hobbling arrival of this suddenly old stranger startles,
but her cold-air companionship echoes with distant harmonies

and lost relations long strained and soured. Still,
I take the familiar hand, squeeze once for yes, twice no

and listen to the patterned discord of our isolation so like rain,
gliding into an easy banter of half-remembered histories.

No one of us says, this is the last time you see me alive
while spring unfolds in her lush soft petals.

Then I become a wordless shadow of shadows,
a modern-day reaper texting death's final arrival—

seeking companionship, finding no signals, all networks
out of range. No one else grieves what's always been gone.

Each year more desolate, an inching lonely mile, I count twenty reasons we walked that narrow path. Each, a mistake.

MAPS FOR AFTER

Don't worry,
new yellow lines ink
into existence
every second.

So close your eyes,
merge from the left.
Inside the long tunnel
everybody swerves.

The regret highway
of additions, subtractions
for every lane you imagine
and some you haven't.

PAPER TIME MACHINES
(SESTINA FOR THE DECEASED)

She'd been ready to die since the last time we met
nearly twenty years ago, but that doesn't change today.
That's regret for you, soft and subtle, more lullaby than heartbeat.
She predicted her last breath, how it'd gasp and tangle:
the hospital bed, her body an experiment, a bad day too soon. Once
   unstuck,
time blends more than it bends. Now her life unfolds like an origami swan,

all the delicate triangles and creases gone. Still. A paper swan,
but flattened. That's how we all unfold at last, into unmet
nerve bundles. Her synapses stopped. Here, then gone. Unstuck.
I see her everywhere now. Window reflections, shadows. Today
she sent a birthday card. Yesterday she left a tangle
of wires crossed in the basement while her heartbeat

stopped. My ear to the envelope of her last letter, as if her heartbeat
might pulse from wading into those words. Her face wan,
already frail, half gone by the time my response arrived. I can't untangle
the swarming nerves, our unshared stories, the places we never met,

The mail takes only two days
but she's gone like a returned letter. Unopened. Is she stuck

in a Faberge egg, unread, full of blank pages? I'm stuck
rereading our words as winter solstice arrives with its slow heartbeat,
and another year without her starts today.
She told me once that swans
mated for life, explaining something about duty. When we met
again, I was old enough to unlock secrets, to entangle.

Like two bold cygnets that turned to our pens, we tangled
our retold tales. We spoke to make sense of our stuck
stamps and stickers, thick pages. We met
more on paper wings, in a flight of imagination and heartbeat.
Migrating, adrift to a placid lake, each of us a floating swan.
We waited, listened, loved despite inevitable losses—days like today.

In the present tense, I hold her last envelope to today's
light and notice the subtle curl of each letter and tangle,
how her words swirled. There's a formula to the elegant, swan
neck of the signature, that penmanship of hers tucked
somewhere between hurry and grace, a heartbeat
or a breath's distance from the struggle. We once meted

our ironic, sad truths, and the lonely grey day we met mirrored today—
dreary and cool. Now I'm a heartbeat closer to death, whose tangled

grasp ever-nears. To get unstuck, I slip her letters into the lake. They float like swans.

THE PRICE OF A SMALL HOT FIRE

Months ago, she withdrew money from the bank,
itemized parcels of a new backyard. A stone fire-pit,
imagining a little of my space into her own.

But between hospital stays
her body made other plans.

What's left is a paper bag,
a pair of reading glasses,
her green slippers,
a tube of pale lipstick,

and the cash to pay
for one last fire.

GIRL RESCINDS PROMISE NOT TO PLAY WITH LION

Forever ago— two lifetimes, maybe more.
Those strange conversations,
nightmare wishes and an odd yen
for a safe place that never existed.

She spoke of imagined days and idyllic scenes,
fumbling when pressed for details
or asked about exiled families.
She considered his mane smelling of forest,

her head nested in warmth—
how he never once scared her.
She recalled with mathematic precision
the gentleness of his understanding.

Her parents scoffed. Urged her to grow up—
as if one could outgrow kindness. So she packed
everything worth fighting for into a small bag.
Opened the closet door— and ran.

IN HER SHADOW I WALK

A cloak as wide as death
stretched like it always had. Waiting.

I wrapped a warm hand around her cold one.
Unable to speak, shrinking from all I meant to say.

Words bounced like ill-tempered frogs,
jumping in all the wrong directions.

We spun grains of sand into stones and
built a wall to live behind.

Our silences thrived like featherless fledglings—
unfortunate. Misshapen and loud.

I was everything she needed to break
or I was not real.

A choking sleep closed around her, and
in the crystal calm, I knew she was gone.

There were no teeth left in that mouth to bite.
I had nothing to fear, yet shivered.

APPROPRIATE PLACES TO GRIEVE

My heart drops, swells with mud.
Maybe she tells me this from the grave,
like that hawk I saw overhead calling
was a message from her,
and everything traces backwards now.
How many steps before I crash?

In the car with the windows up
my head explodes into the reasons why
I waited months to respond,
months, moments spliced out in a hard edit.

There's an instability to this goodbye
that's not like the years she forgot me,
or the years she grieved someone
who didn't exist.

I was unsure until I saw her again
about the ways she made me from
chalk and cinder, ash and witchcraft—
two sticks tied with a thread of hair.

SPECTRAL GLASS

At the seance, I tremble
from want not fear.

Her name, her name.
Let her be the one who reaches—

but even now, I'm a creature
dependent on invitations.

Others call back, whisk the flame
this way and that, knocking

on predictable doors, reliving
their many happy moments,

offering sound comforts of love.
Ours was the path of lions—

a stark way of loving that required
the resonant distance of claws.

A medium gazes at her crystal, flips another card,
stares into the kaleidoscopic moment

between worlds. She flinches, and I know
the power she senses across the table isn't me.

THE MONSTER SPEAKS (MONOLOGUE)

I feel like the monster here is misrepresented. Like people think they know something about me, but is it reality or are they taking things out of context? That's what I need to get into the open. People know an idea. The symbol. Is it a sympathetic view? (Shrugs). I guess not.

There are a lot of assumptions.

Between the creation and the creator, some of us lose twice. After denial, bargaining, and anger, I get to strangling loss. Tricky, tricky. Not everyone reaches acceptance. (Shakes head).

You get what you get.

I'm primal, and I like it that way, but only Mothers have archetypal influence. No one's out, no one's exempt. They imprint a lens on their creations that frames the world: indifferent, sensitive, uncaring, sentimental. Their vibe feeds the background, fills in shades of grey like filters. We learn through their eyes and experiences. I've never met anyone who didn't believe their mother was beautiful. Tell me, are they? (Scoffs).

Anyone who reads the whole story, which some haven't, learns that the monster isn't who you think it is. Who's to say monsters are all bad?

COMPULSIVE

Need to stop
but can't.
Need to.
Stop. But
can't.
Need
to stop.
Can't
stop
need.

The Price of a Small Hot Fire

MONSTER IN A BAG

Punished and pushed,
she stuffs a black plastic bag
full of paper and clothes.

A short lifetime of things worth saving.
The door closes in her face. She looks down,
stunned, eyeing a plush green Frankenstein.

The stranger behind the door stares. Blinks.
Done in. Afraid. Angry. Turns away.
Maybe they share these thoughts?

Standing motionless on the porch
mapping her next steps, she calculates a plan.
She knows better, but worries.

Pauses at the precipice of unbecoming.
She pulls the stuffed monster from the bag,
certain the value of a toy is breathing without air.

MIRROR WALK

When her expression unfolds on my face
I smile at the awakened ghost.

Pause to capture the hint of her, shimmering
at the base of me like a long inescapable shadow.

Like the rough edge of an infected wound,
she's too tender, too insistent to be scrubbed away.

When her voice cascades from my mouth
I shake, startled at the echoing cadences.

Like maternal debts unpaid, I tally her whispers
in each day, finding bits of her everywhere.

When her gestures move my limbs, I'm a puppet
shrinking into the rhythm of replacement.

The Price of a Small Hot Fire

I wrap myself in her sweater, throw back my head
and laugh with the strength of a hundred of us.

Behind me are a thousand things I'll never say
so forge ahead, ahead. Embrace the gathering moments of alone.

NO DEGREES OF SEPARATION

Fe Fy Fo Fum,
she's the one who taught me to run.

She taught me love like a fairy tale
with dandelion dreams and wishing wells,

to uncover paths and learn to lose,
to seek and hide and watch the moon.

A witch's curse, a monkey's paw
a lucky orphan, a mother's caw.

Because of her I learned to find
tricks to bend the world to rhyme.

Always precious, often good I learned
that safety filled the darkest woods.

Hers, not mine, is the face I find
in photos of a missing time.

The Price of a Small Hot Fire

Goodbye mother, goodbye friend.
I miss you now, and I missed you then.

Pish Posh Criss Cross,
I can't explain this kind of loss.

THE DOCTOR ASKS (INTERVENTIONS)

In the last two weeks, how often have you
noticed pecking sadness, a warm blanket of fatigue
lulling you to stillness, trailing concentration,
random kaleidoscopic thoughts,
forgetfulness or a desire for forgetfulness?

If your mood had a color, would you name it
sunshine yellow, feral gray cat, or bison brown?
Would your theme song be played by piano, bagpipes, or cello?
Would your personality's hairdo be soccer mom, rock star, or beehive?
If you could do anything without consequences,
would you start smoking again or stage a military coup?
Both?

Which phrase best describes your motto:
effort creates destiny, the other shoe always drops,
or nihilo ex nihilo?

If your body had a headline, would it read:
You Won't Believe What She Looks Like Now
or Flag Burner Storms Capital?

Would your secret identity be hoarder,
amateur crime solver, or drug dealer?

If you had a single superpower to rescue you,
would it be mind reading, invisibility, or flight?

GOODBYE GREETINGS

Like a tattoo, she's a trace now.
What remained once at my edges,
now needled to skin.

Unstopped, this bottle of life
drained and dried into too late
words like last rites.

Invisible, she clings and stings,
cloaked in ink where
no walls confine her.

Dreaming in ghosts, whenever
a glass drops or a light winks
I imagine our shadowed hello.

THE OLD CRONE TELLS ME A THOUSAND TRUE THINGS

The witch called me up and said
watch out little one, you're in for trouble.
Long finger wagging in the dark. *History.*

She was cold as the gray lake
and soft as bad fruit with hair like moss
plastered to the sides of her head.

She would've scared me but it felt true.
Look kid, she said, *I know about your mother*
in the hushed voice of someone who did.

She smiled and everything went bright—
I fell into the shadow dream of her forest-house,
where tears pooled into gingerbread dreams.

We scratched recipes into the walls of her kitchen,
and I promised to stay until I knew them all by heart.
I worked the soil by hand while we hummed,

turning fallow fields into fecund gardens.

She never hid the keys or locked the gates.

I stayed because I had so much to learn.

FORGIVENESS

The river I wade into has a surprising undertow
licking my ankles into welts.

I sit in the tide and watch the slick waves wash
over my waist, my chest, my shoulders.

This isn't how I learned to survive.
I take a deep breath as water slaps my chin.

I close my eyes, aware
this is how I lose.

UNFINISHED (ARTS AND CRAFTS)

Folded projects in blue plastic bags.
Half a spool of yellow yarn.
Bundles of bright embroidery thread.
Nothing that matches anything about me.

Which is to say, these are her approved colors.
Like them or not, he drops off the bag.
Not a question.
As if to say, please help with what's left.

I pick up the needles. Knit one, purl two.
I complete rows, making each speak,
like small conversations we never had.
We were incomplete.

I don't count the stitches like she would have.
I guess. Make do. Finish gifts to her friends.
As if, as if. We might have said such things.
I am still half of her. Undone.

SHADOW PUPPET

A chimera, shapeshifting into radical formlessness
twisting and transgressive ahead of me

so far as the light could reach. Mythic,
her slender bent arms like willow branches

twisting at impossible angles
blurring around me.

I moved from the source
and she became practically invisible.

We slid into a disrupted stillness:
the maker and the made.

Drunk on equanimity and stillness
she vanished at the fine peak of day.

I inched away, swallowed years like miles
scrambled into the stuff of not paying attention,

ignored the aching tug of strings until I knew

pain was just the color of my bones.

ALTERNATE ENDINGS

True, I unfolded into something that was not a flower,
something nearly unpleasant, but not quite obscene.

I grew like an unfamiliar stretch of road that winds too tight,
a narrow pitch of steep edge where the curve bends
and nerves threaten without really meaning to.

These were the thoughts I had driving to the funeral home.

I'm not the one she wished for, imagined
and nurtured like a plant. I'm the other one.
The one she forgot. More precisely, ignored.
Like a forest in flames, I'm what went wild.

Perspective is everything.

She speaks to me incessantly now. In whispers,
flickering candles. I welcome these ghosts of memory
and dreams where we laugh as hard as when I was easier—
her thing to manage. Something no taller than her waist,
a bundle of hopes small enough to carry like twigs to the fire.

LISTENING GHOST

Umbra, shadow self
listening ghost, mother—

every breeze contains her now,
every found blue feather a message

I place on grief's remembering alter.
The stones of us build a cairn

to guide me. I remember mostly
good things now, and ink out

the ways I hurt—correction—
she hurt me.

Blue jay, I am lonely.
Tell me— is she here?

BLINK

The street we drove, radio on.
Windows down, arms catching breeze
air thick with dust.

A decade ago. Two.
When we were so less careful
about our edges.

At dusk we gathered leaves,
waded knee deep in brown muck,
water soaking our cutoffs with dots of mud.

I speed up until hard memories soften,
become kinder, forget myself
to love her more.

OCEANOGRAPHY

Two dreams ago, I saw her face underwater in my hands.
Like amputees reaching for phantom limbs
we fumbled, forgot to gasp for air.

Unreal words thinned us
into a smooth wet fabric
that intoxicated the skin.

Too saturated to breathe, we sank, repeating
bullet hole words in broken bubble language.
I gave up on translation and became a gap,

a vessel of activities and concerns.
Elapsed. Collapsed. I floated to the surface,
she plunged like a sword into a stone.

We sorted into distant reefs, and I woke alone
remembering all I'd forgotten: how love tastes
of saltwater and fire, how easily I burn.

The Price of a Small Hot Fire

SINKHOLE SWALLOWS FUTURE

no precipitating events
prepared any of us
for the vacant lot vacuum

we found here
or rather, discovered
missing

there's no way to describe
the absence
chasm
void
empty
hole
of
this
life.

Would you like to
continue watching
or return to browse?

FROM ASH

Before, I was ash,
jumpstarted in reverse.

I walked backwards in time
to end up here.

Wind and bone.
Sunlight stinging.

A pile of crushed stone,
something to blow away.

An inky shadow and a bright star—

a million light years from now
my echo imprints the sky.

Recall what you thought you knew
about the world, about me. You didn't.

ONE PAPER BAG

Whoever it was on earth
walking, laughing, sneezing
it comes to this.

A bag on the table. Her.
A bag conceals the box.
Her.

A few words about payment.
Expectations. The polite terror
of an awful conversation.

No one prepares you for
someone in a bag. Whatever you
struggled, avoided, feared, loved—

you meet at this fine point,
arrive for a goodbye.
The person. The bag.

ACKNOWLEDGMENTS

Thanks to the editors and publishers at the following journals where these poems originally appeared, sometimes in different versions.

"Confessions of an Avon Lady's Daughter," *More Queer Families*

"Cherry Blossoms," *HWA Poetry Showcase VIII*, reprinted in the 2022 *Rhysling Anthology*

"Trimurti," *Birthing Monsters*

"Returning to Narnia," *NonBinary Review*

"Sinkhole Swallows Future," *Literary Hatchet*

"One Paper Bag," "From Ash," and "Goodbye Greetings" *The Sirens Call ezine*

E.F. Schraeder

ABOUT THE AUTHOR

Co-editor of the feminist horror charity anthology *In Trouble* (Omnium Gatherum 2023), E.F. Schraeder is the author of the Imadjinn Award finalist book *Liar: Memoir of a Haunting* (Omnium Gatherum, 2021) and other works. Schraeder's poetry, short fiction, and nonfiction have appeared in a number of journals and anthologies. A former gender studies professor, Schraeder holds an interdisciplinary Ph.D. and an advanced degree in Library Science. *The Price of a Small Hot Fire* will be Dr. Schraeder's first full-length collection of poetry.

www.ingramcontent.com/pod-product-compliance
Lightning Source LLC
LaVergne TN
LVHW041201080426
835511LV00006B/693